ISBN 978-1-330-16762-5
PIBN 10042832

FB &c Ltd, Dalton House, 60 Windsor Avenue, London, SW19 2RR.
Company number 08720141. Registered in England and Wales.

For support please visit www.forgottenbooks.com

EDWARD BOND FOOTE

BIOGRAPHICAL NOTES AND APPRECIATIVES

FREE SPEECH LEAGUE
56 East 59th Street
NEW YORK CITY
1913

PRINTED AT HILLACRE
RIVERSIDE, CONNECTICUT

TABLE OF CONTENTS

This volume is prepared by the Free Speech League for the purpose of preserving some tributes to the memory of Dr. Edward Bond Foote, and is for distribution among his friends, in the hope that by thus giving publicity to the splendid service rendered to society by one of its least pretentious and most modest members, others may be encouraged to follow his example.

Theodore Schroeder,

Secretary F. S. L.

DR. EDWARD BOND FOOTE

The all-pervading law of compensation exacts its price, even for the good fortune of having a distinguished parent. In the case of Dr. Edward Bond Foote, the price of such a sire was the temporary overshadowing of his own abilities, at least so far as public recognition was concerned. But he was naturally so unassuming and so intellectually sensitive to and appreciative of those characteristics of his father which had won wide esteem, that in the son's estimation the price was inconsiderable compared with the advantage.

Dr. Ned, as his friends familiarly called him and as I still prefer to call him, was entering upon manhood about the time that his father, Dr. Edward Bliss Foote, came under the influence of that liberal Unitarian, Rev. O. B. Frothingham, and together the father and son traveled the road from Unitarianism to Agnosticism. As with all fundamental thinkers, no subject eventually escaped the scrutiny inspired by the sceptical attitude of mind. Although licensed physicians, both father and son were consistent opponents of "State medicine" and this naturally did not increase their popularity in their profession. They believed sincerely in the popularization of medical science and from this and their religious heresies there was a normal and wholesome growth toward the broadest appreciation of intellectual freedom in general. Libertarian principles gradually became the controlling factor in Dr. Ned's life and it was not long before their importance was indelibly impressed upon his mind.

The initial efforts towards censorship of sex literature under the ban of that plausible, question-begging epithet "obscene" were made in the years 1872 and 1873. The elder Dr. Foote offered some unavailing remonstrance which ensured him the enmity of the influential fellowship of moralists for revenue. He believed he had a constitutional right to spread intelligence, even about sexual subjects, and so risked violation of a law whose criteria of guilt no one knows to this day. Relying upon his assumed rights, he sent to an enquirer a leaflet on the means for promoting "race suicide" and for that reason was arrested and convicted under the postal censorship statute.

About this time Dr. Ned graduated with honors from the College of Physicians and Surgeons and with his father founded and edited *Dr. Foote's Health Monthly*. Through some twenty volumes of this publication the battles for freedom were consistently and courageously waged. Here an extraordinary number of reforms, some of which have since become popular, were given their earliest friendly publicity in some brief notice or review calculated to stimulate interest and a hospitable attitude of mind. There was frequent reference to single tax, spelling reform, free thought, dress reform, the abolition of interest, the promotion of Malthusianism, cremation, prison reform, suffrage, woman's property rights, suggestive therapeutics, greenbackism, food adulteration, medical despotism, the relation of economics to crime and the application of medicine and surgery to the prevention of crime, venereal infection through the drinking cup, vivisection—practically every phase of human interest tending toward freedom and progress, though the main purpose of the magazine was always the popularization of medical science. Much of this missionary work was supplemented by meetings and the organization of societies for discussion of the various subjects, to many of which both father and son contributed financially as well as in time and energy.

The arrest of his father and one other incident of his youth were probably crucial in determining Dr. Ned's later activities. During his tenure as secretary of the New York Liberal Club, a widely advertised lecturer from a distance had at the last moment been unable to keep his appointment and Dr. Ned tried in vain to find a substitute. The other officers of the Club insisted that he should say or read something that would start a discussion and thus avert the probable popular disappointment. He was still too young to have become very proficient as a speaker and there was no time for adequate preparation. He possessed a number of clippings and had made notes on vital subjects which interested him, and from these he hastily prepared a paper which he entitled "Generation Before Regeneration." His audience was obviously divided in its reception of what he had to say even before he had finished speaking, and during the discussion which followed the police arrested several of the "rioters." This incident resulted in the refusal of further use of the college rooms to the Club and eventually in the disruption and death of the organization. Subsequently that paper was published as delivered. To reread it at present is to see much that is yet needed, and to wonder how it could ever have been the cause of a disturbance. It really embodies the foundation principles of his life work. Viewed in long perspective we can see that intellectual hospitality has grown since that paper was read.

After the disruption of the New York Liberal Club, Dr. Foote with his unusual tact and energy gathered together its more radical members and with these organized the Manhattan Liberal Club of which Horace Greeley was the first president. In his maturer years Dr. Ned succeeded Mr. Greeley in the presidential office and for nearly a third of a century this organization offered a platform for the presentation of the most radical thought of the metropolis. Many a noted reformer of our time is, intellectually, a child of that most useful organization and many more owe their intellectual breadth and hospitality to some acquaintance with it. It is probable that the broadening influence of this organization had much to do in developing Dr. Foote's sympathy for liberty from a personal interest to the recognition of a general principle to which all particulars are subordinate.

Late in the seventies Dr. Ned again found himself waging the battle of freedom, but this time among liberals many of whom unfortunately had little knowledge of the principles which were implied in their professed ideals. The censorial laws enacted earlier in the decade were now being vigorously enforced against social heretics and in such a manner as to be specially oppressive to free-thinkers. D. M. Bennett, the editor of the *Truthseeker*, had been arrested for mailing "An Open Letter to Jesus Christ" and "How Do Marsupials Propagate." Ezra Haywood, editor of *The Word*, had been arrested for selling "Cupid's Yokes," Frank Rivers for disposing of "Fruits of Philosophy." Anthony Comstock, at that time the most efficient persecutor, had threatened the suppression of the *Boston Investigator*, the *Truthseeker* and the *Banner of Light*, the first two being free-thought papers and the last a spiritualist organ. In his report for the year 1878 to the "New York Society for the Suppression of Vice," Mr. Comstock had boasted that "another class of publications issued by free-lovers and free-thinkers is in a fair way of being stamped out." If the statutory word "indecent" was not sufficient to actually suppress all free-thought publications, there was a fair prospect of a statutory amendment to include "blasphemy" among the prohibited mail matter.

This naturally alarmed the liberals of the country and soon secured the attention of the National Liberal League, which was then becoming an influential organization. A petition was framed claiming to have seventy-five thousand signatures and praying for "the repeal or modification" of the obscenity laws. Dr. E. B. Foote, Jr., A. E. Giles and J. B. Wolf supported the petition before a congressional committee while Anthony Comstock and Samuel Colgate made successful resistance. Colonel Robert G. Ingersoll did not at first actively appear in support of the petition but favored "modification" of the laws so as to preclude the prosecution of books honestly intended to benefit mankind. For this reason he consented to attach his name to the petition. This brought upon him such virulence of attack from the clergy and other professional moralists that he was frequently impelled to a vigorous disclaimer of any desire for actual repeal of these "obscenity" laws.

This situation brought on a series of conflicts within the National Liberal League between those who desired the repeal and those who were content with little or no modification of the statutes, which conflict finally resulted in the disruption of the League. I think I may roughly classify the contestants into three groups, one of which, headed by the Honorable E. P. Hurlbut, frankly endorsed comstockery and its censorship.

Another was headed by Colonel Ingersoll, who evidently did not believe in complete intellectual freedom as a principle, probably because against the seeming benefits of a particular suppression he did not balance the evils of conceding an unlimited constitutional authority for creating other censorships. This faction demanded a precise definition of the offence and amendments to enlarge liberty to a point of assuring their own safety. Objection to repeal was based only on the desirability of particular suppressions, and on this Colonel Ingersoll argued that: "You cannot afford to put into the mouth of theology a perpetual and continual slur," by failing to appear on record as opposed to the repeal of the "obscenity" statutes. It is regrettable that he was not better informed on the psychology of modesty and obscenity, because with that knowledge and his libertarian tendency he probably would have reached a different conclusion. However, since sexual psychology had not yet been born into the family of sciences, this matter could hardly have been different. Even those who were more radical are found to be similarly hampered.

A third group was led toward a repeal of the federal statutes upon this subject of obscenity under the guidance of D. M. Bennett who seemed to have had even less conception of the principle of freedom than the followers of Ingersoll. Bennett argued that "It is under state laws that obscenity is a crime and *should be punished,*" which position suggests a hypocritical deprecation of "obscene" literature. So far as one can judge at this distance, the motive by which this group was actuated was a belief that state courts would deal more gently with offenders than did federal courts and might be more responsive to that public opinion to which the fanatic Comstockians are, after all, an exception.

The most intelligent advocate of repeal was Thaddeus Burr Wakeman. Although not so popular an orator as Ingersoll, he was a man of greater philosophic attainment and a very forceful speaker in his way. Professor Wakeman stood for repeal on the ground that the statute was unconstitutional. In his Faneuil Hall speech he left little that could comfort any Comstockian. In later speeches he made more definite concessions for the suppression of "obscenity" by the States. The followers of Bennett and Wakeman constituted a majority of the convention. In consequence Ingersoll resigned his vice-presidency and with his followers abandoned the League. But the vanity of respectability apparently with a consciousness of inability to adequately defend general intellectual freedom against the slurs of orthodoxy, induced the mass of liberals to follow Ingersoll rather than Wakeman. A number of Professor Wakeman's addresses attacking the censorship upon constitutional grounds were published by the Doctors Foote. It was no doubt during these years of stress and storm among the liberals that Dr. Ned's own views were crystallizing into those broader principles which he came to see with increasing clarity as one persecution after another elicited his interest and became coördinated in his mind with other like experiences.

The arrest of Bennett and Heywood was followed by the cases of Lant, Train, Slenker, Waisbrooker, Caldwell, Jones, Shew, Thrall, McNair, Noyes, Isaacs and others, each making among liberal-minded people some little stir in its time. The numerous arrests of Moses Harman specially interested Dr. Ned. In every instance where serious opinions were involved in the suppression, he and his father gave needed publicity in their magazine and this without regard to their approval of the suppressed idea. When occasion required it they contributed defense-money. Later they organized a "Defense Committee" which developed into the "National Defence Association," for both of which the *Health Monthly* was the unofficial organ.

Dr. Ned was the treasurer of many similar liberalizing organizations, often making the initial contribution and providing for the final deficit after others had wearied of giving. I remember he told me on one occasion that he felt he ought to make some report as treasurer of a certain organization but that he really was ashamed to do so because the contributions other than his own were so small and so few. Such was the inherent modesty of this extraordinary man.

When impossible for him to appear personally before legislative committees having under consideration laws for the further curtailment of liberty, especially in the dissemination of knowledge upon vital human affairs, Dr. Ned would finance a representative Thus he took an active part in every important struggle for larger intellectual freedom that occurred during his mature life and always with that characteristic self-abnegation which made him content to fight without reward or glory, or even recognition, though he never shrank from work in the vanguard when such heroism was demanded.

Of course neither Dr. Foote nor the little group of courageous fighters inspired by him could expect to really thwart the lust for power and greed for pelf which impel increasingly invasive legislation, and despite their ceaseless resistance our censorship of opinion has grown apace with all our other forms of paternalism. The glory of their work is not in the achievement but in the fine impersonal character of the effort.

The popular hysteria aroused by the assassination of President McKinley led to the passage of numerous "anti-anarchist" laws which if uniformly enforced would certainly have excluded from the United States even such characters as Tolstoi and Jesus. When an English anarchist named John Turner was arrested here for deportation it was decided by the friends of free speech to test the constitutionality of such legislation. A voluntary association was formed and called "The Free Speech League" and as usual Dr. Ned was made treasurer It was in this capacity that he did a fine thing characteristic of the genuineness and courage of the man. At that time the "yellow" journals had made some leaders of the anarchist group of America the most widely feared and despised persons in the United States and of course these were terribly hounded by the police and through them by the landlords. Dr. Foote did not agree with their social theories, but, as a libertarian, he felt that they had a right to disagree with him and with others and to be protected in expressing those theories. As the surest protection which he could give and with no concern whatever for his own popularity or comfort, he aided the leader of them to secure employment as a nurse to one of his patients and coöperated with her for the preparation and financing of the Turner defence.

It was in actions such as this that the broadness and heroism of Dr. Ned's intellectual hospitality were constantly shown. Wherever men and women were persecuted for their beliefs, however unpopular, he was always generous in their defence. In many instances where imprisonment followed, he even contributed to the support of the prisoner's family during incarceration. He seemed to feel almost a personal responsibility for any abridgement of human liberty and was ready to expend himself to the uttermost to right such wrongs done by society toward its heretics whether friends or strangers, whether holding opinions with which he agreed or those radically opposed. It was precisely in such impersonal services as these in which could not be any possible material advantage, public acclaim or respectable recognition that he deliberately sacrificed both money and popularity. He was contented to devote his whole life to humanitarian effort without even the recognition by others that he had any existence as a humanitarian. Such modesty and such life-long devotion to impersonal service in the promotion of principles are very seldom combined in the same man and evidence the very rarest of virtues. Hoping to perpetuate his efforts for the enlargement of intellectual liberty, he was mainly instrumental in inducing the incorporation of The Free Speech League in 1911.

He often expressed regret that radicals and freethinkers had not developed larger and more efficient institutions for the promotion of human betterment according to their own radical ideals. He had more than once regretted the absence of a pension fund for veterans of unpopular causes. When Professor Wakeman, Colonel Ingersoll and others conceived the idea of a Liberal University at Silverton, Ore., Dr. Ned gave generously toward the enterprise. He heartily approved of the project to teach science and philosophy according to the revelations of the scientific method rather than that expanding minds should be tortured into conformity with alleged revelations from God. Much financial aid had been expected through the efforts of Colonel Ingersoll, whose death, however, intervened to frustrate this part of the plan, and the whole project failed, after a few years of devoted effort. But Dr. Ned's faith never wavered in his confidence in the ultimate value of such a center of liberalized learning and the fine influence it would eventually have upon the educators of the country.

Every little while it was his custom to distribute money for the promotion of humanitarian ends. No one organization received enough at one time to furnish spectacular headlines in the newspapers, but he probably gave most of his earnings. Perhaps not even his best friends knew all the diversified humanizing efforts which he helped. Freethinkers knew one side, freespeakers another; eugenists another; single-taxers, medical reformers, anti-vaccinationists, legitimationists knew still other sides and so on down the list even to spelling reformers and conventional philanthropists. No one will know all. Even during his last illness he did not forget his wards. The following list represents part of the institutions to whose work he contributed and is given as illustrative of his broad sympathy: Paine National Historical Society; Society for Ethical Culture, Summer Home; New Rochelle Hospital; Fels Fund of America; Free Speech League; Washington Square House for Friendless Girls; Mothers' and Babies' Committee of the State Charities Aid Committee; New York Child Labor Committee;

Brooklyn Affiliated Charities; American Seaman's Friends Society; Association for Practical Housekeeping, George Republic; Men's League for Women's Suffrage; American Secular Union; Berkshire Farm Association; New York Probation Association; Brooklyn Bureau of Charities; Parks and Playground Association; Children's Aid Society, for Fresh Air Fund; Prison Association of New York; National Purity Association; Free Thought Tract Society; Postal Reform League and Charity Organization Society. All this besides many contributions to radical and free thought publications. If specifically libertarian organizations are not as predominant in the above list as might be wished, the explanation may be found in their inefficiency. Even here we see a fine impersonal spirit manifested in that Dr. Foote was unwilling to be released from well-doing, merely because he was unable to exhaust his powers in what seemed to him preferable objects and methods. If he could not do good in his own best way he would do it according to another's way, but always do the best possible under given circumstances.

Dr. Foote was a sincere and zealous Malthusian who considered it an outrage to allow children to be born into unfit environment, or as unwelcome guests or from physically unfit parents simply because legalized bigotry makes it a crime to give information as to means for avoiding fecundation. Here he practised what he preached in a fine devotion to principle. In the most impersonal manner he estimated his own physical unfitness for parenthood, generously resolving all doubts against himself and in favor of the potential offspring. With a like sensitive regard for the happiness of others he hesitated to inflict so deep a deprivation upon another and consequently refrained from marriage until late in life.

So without the blessings of offspring, though under the zealous and intelligent devotion and tender ministrations of his wife, Dr. Mary E. Bond Foote, Dr. Ned's life passed peacefully and painlessly away, she prolonging his services to humanity by executing his wishes in the socially useful distribution of his estate.

He was preëminently a humanitarian in the very best and broadest sense. From infancy he breathed the atmosphere of protest against tyranny—the tyranny of fear, of superstition, of disease, of injustice, of poverty, of ignorance. He labored ceaselessly to dissipate the fogs of mystery by spreading the light of science. He had chosen a profession which, in its finer aspects, is a profession of service and he sought to popularize its attainments. By the revisions of his father's books he literally made them his own. Through this form of popularized science the humanitarian effort of his career brought him into helpful relations with literally over a million of suffering humans. I think the fundamental and guiding principle of his life was the insistence that every one should have an acknowledged right to know all that is to be known upon every conceivable subject, for thus only can we preserve for all an equal and fair opportunity in life.

As a political heretic, early identified with progressive movements whose policies are only now attaining popular recognition, he grew to ideals still more radical. He was among the pioneers in every effort to promote social justice such as those looking toward the creation of Eugenic Science, the teaching of sex hygiene in the public schools, the promotion of race betterment through intelligent sex selection, the voluntary sterilization of defectives; uncoerced enlightened maternity and childhood and motherhood welfare in general. In this connection he anticipated much of the recent thought by which we are developing a scientific moral code, especially in relation to sex.

He made much money, spent on himself only enough to live in refined simplicity and considered all the rest as held in trust for humanity. Perhaps even this is not so unusual as to elicit very great homage unless we take into account the tender yet enlightened sympathy which prompted all, the refined sense of justice which guided him to seek and befriend the most unpopular of the victims of the most conspicuous pharisees. Thus he sought to balance the scales of justice even for the most despised, especially if they were such as are usually neglected by professional philanthropists or most scorned by the conventionally self-righteous.

In enlightened circles, culture is measured by the extension of the field of consciousness of social relations. Judged by this test Dr. Edward Bond Foote was one of the most cultured among men. He had a conscious kinship to all humanity. A wrong to any one, anywhere, was a wrong to himself by virtue of his own kinship to all the rest. He not only sympathized with and understood the sufferings and needs of the oppressed, but what is more important, he also understood the oppressor, and so could be hurt without being revengeful, could seek restraint and cure without desiring to inflict punishment, and could be kind and generous without being self-righteous. Furthermore, this was not a mere matter of sentimentalism but rather of intelligent comprehension of social relations and causation. Where others dispense charity to those whose bodies are in need, he cured the body and sought to bestow his surplus wealth where it would feed the mind rather than the stomach, or the stomach that had a socially useful mind above it. When others saw only the individual sufferer he saw also the relation of that suffering to its causes in human ignorance, perverse social conventions and institutions. Where others only attempted to relieve pain, he endeavored to remove the personal and social causes of pain. Where others sentimentalized he rationalized. Where some are content to bestow their benefactions only upon those who can applaud within hearing, this man without ostentation gave a helping hand to every new idea seeking a rational expression, no matter who or where on earth its advocate might be. In this sense it is literally true that he gave substantial aid to intellectual and social progress all over the world. He was not content that superficially all should appear to have an equal chance, he sought to insure them also the *best* equal chance.

He lived, he worked, he suffered, that others in the future might live richer and happier lives than those of the past. Almost the only joys of his life, certainly the greatest joys of his life, came through making others happy. There is perhaps no surer, saner way to make the world a better place to live in, few if any greater or more far-reaching forces for human betterment as a whole, than the practice of such sweet tolerance as his for those who differ, his calm resignation both in triumph and disaster, and his gentle yet ceaseless devotion to the truth, for humanity's sake.

THEODORE SCHROEDER

At a memorial meeting held December 22. 1912, in Bryant Hall, New York City, the following addresses were made and letters read in appreciation of the character and service of Dr. Edward Bond Foote.

ADDRESS BY

PROF. THADDEUS B. WAKEMAN

(Author and Lawyer)

"The longer we live and the more we learn, the more certain we are of one thing and this is that practically all of the ills that mankind is supposed to inherit may be greatly mitigated, even entirely eliminated, through knowledge and the proper application of that knowledge. Even calamities that are blasting, final, such as war and death, when seen in their relation to the whole human world often become the conditions of life's chiefest blessings—a new man, a new nation, seeking a higher purpose.

"It was so at the close of the Civil War in 1865. It was then that our thinkers began to seriously consider what the blood-and-death-bought future and promise of the American people should be. A deep and widespread wave of religious feeling swept over the country, springing from an entirely new source—no longer that of other-world revelation but born of a sense of social service based upon social science and an intelligent appreciation of the import of true religion and the needs of the nation as a whole.

"On this foundation and for these purposes a number of organizations were formed, particularly in our Northern States. Some of these were very broad in their teaching, as broad as the movement of Positivism in France, and Herbert Spencer's philosophy of evolution in England. A new and widespread conviction came into being in this country, to the effect that the old bases of religion would no longer stand the test which the newer science and democracy would apply to it.

"The result was a number of organizations for liberal discussion as well as scientific associations, chief among which and in a sense combining the several purposes of both, was *The* Liberal Club of New York. At the beginning this had only about half a dozen members, but soon something like a score began meeting in a Third Avenue restaurant and later in Plympton Hall, then at 141 Sixth Street, which they converted into "Science Hall." The Club was inaugurated on the fourteenth of September, 1869, on the occasion of a Great Humboldt birthday celebration. It was later incorporated and for about thirty years held meetings every Friday night for public discussion, in addition to dinners, exhibitions and meetings for special discussions and the consideration of important subjects, as occasion demanded.

"The main object of the Liberal Club is stated in my certificate of membership which I have here in my hand—I was one of the first members—'the extension of the study of science, literature and art.' In other words, science stood for truth, literature for general knowledge and information, and art (including the application of truth to life) was extended to cover what we called universal art, from architecture to music, ethics and the entire conduct of civilized life.

"I have a reason for referring to these matters in some detail, for among the first who gathered at the meetings of the Liberal Club was Dr. E. Bliss Foote, already well known as the preacher of health, physical and mental, the editor of the *Health Monthly*. With him, later, came his son, Dr. Edward Bond Foote, whose memorial we are here now to celebrate, and to keep his memory fresh by recalling the facts that gave it value. It was through this Club that 'Dr. Ned Foote, Jr.,' became my personal friend. Almost from the first there was between us a friendship that became increasingly warm and devoted. We had both entered into the Liberal Club movement with all our heart and energy. Dr. Ned had then but recently graduated from the College of Physicians and Surgeons in this city and he poured all the wealth of his youthful enthusiasm and ideals into the work of the Club.

"About the same time he became interested in some liberal and religious movements along other lines and frequently listened to the preaching of Mr. O. B. Frothingham, a well-known liberal Unitarian minister. But it was in the Club that he took, as he laughingly claimed, the two positions of postgraduate student and also teacher from the medical university—a humorous instructor when he could teach, a serious teacher when he could learn.

"He was also a member of and a worker with nearly every liberal movement promising anything good or progressive in this city, from that time until the day of his death. It was for this reason that in his compilation and writing of that very useful work. 'Four Hundred Years of Free Thought,' the late Samuel P. Putnam obtained from Dr. Foote a short statement of his life and views. That was in 1894, when this book was published by the *Truth Seeker.* He then put himself on record, as it were, so that we have there a complete résumé of his judgment, his views, purposes and life. I want to read from that short statement that he then made for all and so for us. It gives in his own words the picture of his work and his hopes when in his prime:

" 'It makes me feel rather lonesome to build my platform, and I even wonder whether I may not have to occupy it all alone. If there be others cast to fit this mold, just like me, I should be glad to know where to find them, though I am far from wishing that every one should agree with me all round. In medicine I am eclectic, with preference for hygienic practice, but a believer in utility of medicine; an advocate of medical freedom, or abrogation of all restrictive laws that rule out undiplomaed 'healers'; an anti-vaccionationist, but a believer in utility of vivisection *limited.* As a hygienist I favor (and almost practice) vegetarianism, avoid tobacco, and apply prohibition of alcoholics to myself. I am one of the neo-malthusian cranks who would limit population, and my pet hobby is 'eugenics,' or the right of every child to be well born, or not at all. So I also advocate woman suffrage, and the sexual emancipation of women, less *bondage* in marriage, far greater freedom in divorce, and believe that every child should be as *legitimate in law as in nature.* Politically I favor Nationalism, or the People's Party, a moderate protective tariff, bimetallism on the old basis (for the present), and greenbackism as soon as we can be freed from barbarous devotion to metals.

" 'As to religion, I am Agnostic, subscribe to the articles of the Secularists, and find myself pretty closely in accord with the Positivism of Mr. T. B. Wakeman, to whom I am glad of an opportunity to offer publicly many thanks for much useful, rational, liberal instruction. Lastly, I look forward to cremation, and anticipate nothing further, except the continuing results of my life, works and influence.'

"In this statement we have a man modestly revealing to us as perfect a humanitarian, as alert and progressive a physician, as vigorous and fearless a reformer, as any man in New York City, perhaps in any city. And among us who survive and who are rallying about the colors since he left the ranks, how many of us measure up to his standard in real liberality, courage and simple, unostentatious beneficence?

"It is impossible, of course, to give here and now the full facts, the countless personal details that richly justify this highest praise. But all you who now hear me speak, know it to be true. Those who will follow me on this platform to-day in giving Dr. Foote's service and character the tribute they deserve, are but a handful of the thousands who could bear witness to the influence his life has had upon the cause of liberal thought and progress along every line throughout this country.

"As a man, Dr. Foote was so modest and retiring that to the multitude, even among his beneficiaries, he is scarcely known. He was so unpretentious and unaggressive that individuals and the public alike forgot to repay him for labor and means expended for their benefit. He literally devoted his time, his energy, his life to the cause of human liberty that was so dear to his heart. If any man ever deserved blessing or recognition for his benefactions, our deceased friend deserves these of us, and that our appreciation should impel us to continue the good work and the high principles that were the dominating factors of his life.

"There is one fact that I want to impress upon you—leave with you—and that is, that of the Old Guard Liberals only a few of us are now left. It should be our main purpose, our sole aim, to so impress the meaning of liberality upon those about us that when we at last lay down our arms there shall arise a host to follow in our footsteps and fight in our places for the cause that is dear to our hearts.

"If we are makers of money, very well. Let us make it and also use it as did our fallen comrade, for the good of all. I recall that I was with him in that last attempt for a Liberal University—a movement that gained a footing then and can yet, I believe, be brought to a successful fruition. Those charters obtained in the States of Missouri and Oregon are still alive and can be used to organize and continue the work which Dr. Foote, Colonel Ingersoll and others then inaugurated. Rational human progress demands that such universities be opened as a practical means of putting all science at the service of humanity, of making science the basis of human life and action and that there may be trained men and women everywhere to carry on the work of secular education in a rational, liberal way.

"Every Liberal should be ashamed that heretofore all efforts toward such fundamental, radical enlightenment of mankind should have fallen short, come to naught, for want of properly equipped, adequately trained men and women, no less than for means to thus uphold the standard of truth. It is in such times that we feel most sorely the loss of such men as the one we honor to-day. Dr. Foote, with Colonel Ingersoll, Courtland Palmer—men whose lives, could they have been continued but a few years longer, would have notably advanced the new education and the progress of the world

—literally gave their lives to the Liberal cause. If only their scientific methods and their zeal can be continued, the cause will still live and will become the impetus of a new era of peace and progress and human welfare not only in the history of this country but in the story of humanity as a whole.

"It is with us that our dead friend, Dr. Foote, has left this cause that was so dear to him. It is for us, for you here before me, to supply the men and women and the means to carry it on. Our love for him could raise to him no more acceptable monument than new leaders to continue his work—men who can take his place and complete his great aim and realize the great end which the Old Guard of the Liberals originated. This is the work I leave with you—the present and the rising generation."

ADDRESS BY BOLTON HALL

(Lawyer and Author)

"You perhaps remember that poem of Maeterlinck's—for it is no less a poem than a drama—in which he makes the children, seeing again their grandparents, childishly and frankly say that they had supposed that the old people were dead. And then the grandparents say, 'No, we are not dead; so long as any one speaks of us we live' I have sometimes thought that that is really symbolic of life, that perhaps as we look in our cemeteries at the tablets of stone or bronze, it is not these that perpetuate our deeds, but that as long as there is any memory of those whose remains lie mouldering underneath, as long as the name Robert Ingersoll or Henry George or Henry Ward Beecher carries to the minds of men some thought of what manner of man this was, what he did, what he thought, what he gave his life for, so long in every recurrent mention of the name, in every recurring thought of the person, that person still lives.

"And again in the same poem or drama we have that clear vision that enables a poet to crystallize discussions and sayings, when the children go to the graveyard together and the graves open. Instead of the pallid corpses or the pale ghosts that the children expected to see, nothing appears and the children say one to the other, 'Why, there are no dead.'

"Practical religion, such as Mr. Wakeman has been telling us about, and practical science alike, teach us that there are no dead.

"We have seen life, an endless flux and reflux of life, an endless repetition, not of death but of revivification. We have seen how things that we have been accustomed to think of as inert matter—the mineral kingdom—are really throbbing and thrilling with the same crystallizing, thought-producing, life-bearing energy that inspires and moves the whole world. We know how the dead silex as it lies in the field is taken up and made to form the hardness and the stiffness of the stem and the grain of wheat; taking what we have thought of as dead to form life—vegetable life. We have seen how the grain in turn ministers to human life, passes into our frames and becomes the hardness and stiffness of our bones. The mineral life passes into vegetable life and the vegetable life into animal life by insensible processes, so that no man can say where death ends and life begins; and the process still goes on until we are again gathered to our mother, the earth, and the unceasing round begins again, when that which was alive turns once more into material like the sandy silex and wheels once more its round.

"We look at the mineral kingdom and we say nothing is dead; then we look at the vegetable kingdom and we say there are no dead; and we look at that which endures of our departed friend—till we can almost see that Spirit rise to-day among us, and we say there is no death. Yet I know there is the human grief, the desolation, the empty longing arms and the breast that aches for the dear familiar weight.

"For these philosophy is in vain; these nothing helps at all but Love—that Love that we come here to-day to show forth as best we may. So I only suggest these religious thoughts (because philosophy and religion are one), well knowing that words are helpless, helpless to change the course of destiny, helpless to bring back to us the person and the face that we so sadly miss.

"Yet what is it, after all, that we miss? What is it but the warm touch of the hands and the warm feel of the arms? What is that thing that lived with us before we came to the grave and that goes home with us afterwards? It is that kindliness, that thought, that affection which are indeed the very spirit of our dead friend. That thing which has its influence, which does not depend upon the warmth of the body for immortality, an immortality which does not even depend upon the memory of man for its being nor upon the body for its life, that true thought, that kind word, that gentle look, that loving heart, which though invisible can never die, as Love can never die.

"So we came here to speak not only in

general terms but in personal, particular ways of one of whom and to whom these ideas more than to others were living, vital truths—Dr. Foote. He was devoted to the cause of free speech, free thought and free life, although not an aggressive man and well aware of the dangers of his course, yet he went on and worked on unshaken.

"It is told of Napoleon that as he sat on horseback watching his troops riding into action there was many a laugh or light word from the lips of those who rode, but one young officer passed, holding tight to his horse, pale, and with his lips trembling. Some of the officers sneeringly said, 'There goes a man that is afraid.' 'No,' said Napoleon, 'there goes the bravest man in my army. He knows the danger, but he goes on.'

"And so it was with Dr. Foote. A man of naturally nervous temperament, I remember how he came to me once for some legal help because he had received a decoy letter from the unspeakable Comstock Society, and I remember very well the timorousness and the trepidation with which he spoke about this thing and the danger to his work and activities. Then I remember still better how many a man has been led aside by that most specious of arguments, 'Let me preserve my standing, let me keep my platform.' Many a man would have said, 'This is not the time to appear in radical things or to be forward in reform; it would be wise to wait a little and let things quiet down.' But not so at all with Dr. Foote, his force and his purse were as much at the disposal, more at the disposal, of the needy, much maligned cause than before this attempted persecution had begun. And what Napoleon said, 'There goes a man who knows the danger and still goes on,' recurred to me as I talked with Dr. Foote. This was a man who understood the fundamentals of reform, the reform that must begin with free speech; that thing which is at the base of all other reforms, that men shall be able to communicate freely with each other, that which the Spirit has communicated to them; a man who saw how all-important it is that all men should be able to preach and to teach the Kingdom of God that is within them."

ADDRESS BY JAMES F. MORTON

(Lawyer and Editor)

"The last time I stood upon this platform it was to bear my share of tribute to Moses Harman, one of the pioneers in the movement for human purity, human progress; and our meeting to-day is to draw closer the memories that cluster about one of the other workers, one of the foremost workers in that same vital cause, Dr. Edward Bond Foote.

"Dr. Foote was one of the cleanest-minded men whom I have ever known. In the deepest and most intimate sense, he never treated the subject of sex in a trivial or flippant manner. As a matter of course, being one of the cleanest and purest-minded of men, he regarded with the abhorrence with which all clean-minded men and women must regard it, any blasphemy against human purity. Dr. Foote looked upon sex as the key to humanity, which should be clean all the way through, clean in body, clean in mind, clean in desire, aspiration, clean in character; and so he believed in the deepest sense in eugenics. If there was any one subject which seemed to dominate his work it was eugenics. Although his heart was open to all liberal causes and as you have heard here to-day his purse was always open and he took a deep interest in every life force which seemed in any way capable of tending toward human progress, yet more than any other the subject of eugenics, in the broadest sense, fitted in with every wish and every interest that lay close to his heart. Not in the sense of the mere passing phase of the hour, before the world for a short time and then to pass in favor of some other fad, but in its deepest and most comprehensive sense, he believed that in order to develop correctly the human race, human beings must be well born, that adverse conditions militate against bringing into the world well-equipped and healthy children; that prenatal conditions influence the personalities to be produced; that all adverse conditions whether they be of the mind or of the body, whether they be economic or psychological or superstitious, the narrowness of prejudice or the littleness of aim or of character, should be eliminated.

"Dr. Foote was indifferent to censure, indifferent even to the censure of those whom he loved but who failed to understand his motives; indifferent to those who take words as representing realities and who in the name of purity persecute and impress. Dr. Foote knew the slanderous and scandalous abuse which all who have been engaged in the wider eugenic movement have been compelled to undergo. Dr. Foote unmasked the hypocrisy that gave Comstock an opportunity to carry on his work by sending, within the past two or three weeks, a committee to the Board of Education denouncing the teaching of sexual hygiene to the teachers in our public schools, declaring that it was opposed to all interests of sexual hygiene, extending beyond the scope of the actually born child. He stood fearlessly for the study of sex, in its fullest meaning. To him sex was power, pure instinct to the intensest degree, as the means by which nature carries on life in everything, in the lives of all beings, from the plant to the human. It was to him intensely pure; it was to be studied —studied carefully, studied earnestly, and was to be taught in the deepest and fullest manner. To him impurity was in the mind of those who feared to teach it. He looked upon sex as he looked upon other manifestations in nature. He was not absorbed in it, with a mind abnormally fixed upon it, having an interest in its outward material expressions to the exclusion of other interests. That is a false idea which has been falsely charged against eugenic reformers in general.

"To Dr. Foote, sex had its proper place in life as it has its proper function with other human functions, and to understand its right relations was to forget that prurient curiosity and that attitude of mind which is so characteristic of our Anglo-Saxon race. To know sex properly is to drop all false prudery and to allow sex education to take its place. So Dr. Foote was a eugenist; he was a neomalthusian as he understood the term, a believer in the intelligent control of the production of the human race; not with merely a few, a limited number of individuals to be determined, but with a realization of the social necessities of the whole for a higher and better civilization. With him it was not how many, but how good; not how numerous, but how in the best and most fit conditions; not quantity, but quality.

"Science is fully disposed to accept pioneer eugenics, and believes that it is more important to the nation, to the community, more important to the whole human race, to have the child born under the best possible conditions, to have the finest type of human being brought into the world; to have the best environment possible for beings born into the world. Science believes that it is best to determine the men and women who are to carry on the work of civilization, believes that this is more important than the mere promiscuous multiplication of human beings, as advocated and practiced by the popular and more or less demagogic methods of our time.

"Dr. Foote was a radical eugenist because he believed in quality more than quantity in that which concerns the human race. Dr. Foote was throughout his life an apostle of sex sanity, sex balance, sex education. He was not an extremist; he believed in truth, in the whole truth; he believed that all those who had any thought to contribute on this most vital subject should be heard. It remains for us to carry on the truth he fought for until the world becomes enlightened and purified and the foundations are well and truly laid for a higher, purer and better development of humanity."

ADDRESS BY LEONARD D. ABBOTT

(Author and Associate Editor of *Current Opinion*)

"We commemorate to-day something that is rare in this world, a man of principle. We also commemorate a philanthropist in the true and original sense of that word—one who loves his fellow man.

"Every great man is many-sided. He cannot be easily summed up. Dr. Foote's activities were felt in many fields. My own most intimate association with him was in connection with the Thomas Paine National Historical Association. That Association was very dear to his heart, and he gave a great deal of money and time to it. Many of those present have seen the little house at New Rochelle in which Thomas Paine lived. Dr. Foote turned it into a Paine museum and set in it a life-sized statue of Paine. W. M. van der Weyde helped in this work, gathering books and making photographs for the museum. I regard this as the most interesting free-thought institution in the country. I think the free-thinkers of America ought to see that this place is preserved in perpetuity. I hope they will.

"Another cause in which Dr. Foote and I were associated was the fight for free speech for Radicals.

"About five years ago a prominent anarchist was giving a lecture in this city. Her meeting was suppressed by the police and her audience driven from the hall. This was one of the most flagrant outrages on free speech of which I know. A committee was formed to defend the rights of the "Queen of anarchism" and of any one else—to utter their convictions in public. Dr. Foote was so concerned in this fight that he offered us his office to meet in. He gave us his counsel and also contributed money. He was one of the factors that finally broke down this police prosecution because he showed the world that there are clean people willing to fight for the rights of even the "most despised."

"Dr. Foote was one of those who were deeply interested in the martyrdom of Francisco Ferrer, the founder of the Modern Schools in Spain. He said, 'It is a new case like that of Giordano Bruno,' and he was right. The killing of Ferrer at Barcelona three years ago was perhaps the most notable case of martyrdom for an idea since Bruno. When a school in memory of Ferrer was started in this city one of the first two financial contributions came from Dr. Foote.

"Then there was the case of Kotoku and the Japanese Anarchists. Twelve Japanese Anarchists were executed in Tokyo in January, 1911, after a secret trial. Their execution took from eight o'clock in the morning until four o'clock in the afternoon. Twelve more were imprisoned for life. The full details of this extraordinary case are not known even yet, but we know that the killing of Kotoku and his comrades was a terrible crime against humanity and against liberty. When a group of radicals were fighting in America to save Kotoku and his comrades from the gallows, Dr. Foote gave his moral and financial support.

"Dr. Foote was interested in the free speech fights conducted by the Industrial Workers of the World in Spokane, in Fresno, California, and other Western cities. He did not always agree with the tactics of the I.W.W., but when the principle of free speech was involved, his time and his purse could be depended on.

"I am glad that the chairman to-day has given me the subject: 'He Defended the Right to Differ.' There are only a few men who are brave enough to defend the right to express opinions they do not agree with, to defend free speech as a principle. Dr. Foote was such a man. He did not ask whether he saw eye to eye with a man before he would help him. He had the large conviction that there could not be real progress in the world unless we each one of us have the undeniable right to express the truth as we see it.

"He is well described as one whose mission was to uproot superstition and to uphold individual liberty."

ADDRESS BY EDWIN C. WALKER

(Author and Editor)

"It seems to me that the five most characteristic elements of Dr. 'Ned' Foote's temperament and intellect were generosity, genial kindliness, a sense of humor, a watchful love of freedom of expression, and judicial fairness.

"Those slim, white fingers were always tempted to slip into the right-hand lower pocket of his waistcoat to draw out a five or ten or twenty for some sufferer or some child of poverty or a cause that was in straits And quite surely he had early learned to act in the spirit of the principle later enunciated by Hugh O. Pentecost, 'The way to overcome temptation is to yield to it.' So the slim, white fingers very, very often had their way and came out attached to a "V" or something larger, for all the one's and two's were in some other pocket, apparently. And when a larger sum was needed or the beneficiary was beyond the reach of the long arm, the check-book lost a leaf.

"This man, so early passed from among us, was the almoner of Liberalism in America. Other men of progressive ideas have had more and a few have given much, but no other, I am convinced, ever has given so frequently, so widely, so timely, and so discriminatingly and justly. His assistance has strengthened many a weary arm, kindled hope anew in many a despairing heart, and renewed the well-nigh exhausted activity of many a tired brain. So often, too, the keen, quaint, "battling" letters that went with the spontaneous gifts were in themselves elixirs of cheer and courage and determination.

"The kindly smile, the quizzical inquiry or assent of the eyes, the genial friendliness of the whole attitude, so familiar to all who knew him, remain among memory's sweetest possessions. He was a most charming companion in automobile trips through the woods or in his launch on the Sound, despite the growing deafness that made conversation extremely difficult in later years, and that toward the last kept him away from nearly all meetings. But wherever he was, the tender smile, the responsive eyes, spoke the language of understanding and comradeship, and so words were not missed so much.

"Our friend's wit and his sense of humor were keen and ebullient. A confirmed punster, he caught every possibility for a "hit." Gentle satire was not a stranger to his tongue or pen, while the enemies of liberty felt often the sting of his sarcasm. He had a pretty fancy for farce with a purpose, as all must confess who experienced the delight of seeing and hearing him at the Manhattan

Liberal Club that night in the dual rôle of Rev. Dr. Parkhurst and himself, turning first one and then the other side to the audience as he carried alone the witty and cutting dialogue.

"His service to the cause of freedom of speech and press was incalculable. His father and himself may almost be said to have been for years the heart and soul and purse of the National Defense Association and the Free Speech League. The so-called Comstock Postal Statutes, enacted in March, 1873, and strengthened later by various amendments, marked not only the beginning of a 'movement in favor of ignorance,' as C. L. James tersely described it, but also a movement in favor of disease, the deeper subjection of wives, of abortion, and undesired and misery-destined children. The senior Dr. Foote was early a victim of the Censor's density or malice, and during all their after years, father and son lived in constant apprehension of the destruction of their publishing plant, the strangling of their great enterprise of enlightenment and humanity. But neither faltered in his work, and they left a legacy of devotion and money that still is supporting and long will support the cause they loved and served while living.

"To Moses Harman, they and other men of means they enlisted for the campaign against medievalism, gave much money and immeasurably valuable moral assistance. It is no disparagement of the zeal and helpfulness of his other friends to say that Harman, in all probability, would have been beaten to the earth long before his heroic struggle ended in death had it not been for the upholding hands of Dr. Ned Foote. Anarchists and other assailed reformers have much reason to remember him with respect and gratitude. His first question was not, 'Do I accept all this man or woman is trying to teach?' but, 'Has he or she the right to endeavor to change the opinions of others through peaceful instruction and is the exercise of that right denied?' He knew that many propagandists would say, were saying, foolish things, but he knew also that the best answer, sometimes the only answer, to their foolishness was the expression of it. He held stanchly that fresh air and sunlight are cheap and excellent disinfectants in the realm of thought as elsewhere.

"It has taken more years to teach some of us than were required in the case of Dr. Foote. I think he was the fairest speaker I have ever heard. At the Manhattan Liberal Club, the Sunrise Club, at meetings in his parlors, and elsewhere, it was quite common in the nineties and even later to cavil at what we called his hair-splitting and fence-balancing. To change from these to another figure, we wanted him to swallow this or that social gospel in bulk, without comparison, analysis, or reservation. The truth is, he was maturing earlier than we were, myself included; he realized sooner that there are at least two sides to every question, that the diamond of truth has many facets, that no person or party is wholly right or wholly wrong, that the social world is kept in its orbit by the constant opposing action of the centripetal and centrifugal forces. So he rarely made an all-around partizan speech—never, perhaps, save when defending freedom of inquiry or inveighing against vaccination—he ever sought to reach a conclusion by a balanced statement of the arguments for and against a proposition. The hesitation we censured as 'weather-vaning' was born, not of timidity, but of a knowledge wider than our own, of a keener realization of two facts—that every effect has many causes, and that every proposed reform, if successful, will only in part realize the dream out of whose womb it came, and among its good results will bring some that are the opposite of good.

"Of course, Dr. Foote was not a pioneer, in the absolute sense, in the movement for the open and thorough discussion of the questions of sex and marriage. To find these, we must go back to Wollstonecraft, Shelley, Godwin, or further yet. But he *was* a pioneer, as contrasted with the multitudes that now are hailed as the pathfinders in eugenics. Beside him, his contemporaries, and their predecessors of the generation before, most of these teachers of to-day are but babes in arms. The vast majority of them do not know it and even some of the survivors of the 'Old Guard' are apt to forget it in their exultation due to the rapid spread of interest in and acceptance of public discussion of marriage and divorce, eugenics and prostitution. What the Chicago *Trib-*

une, the Cincinnati *Commercial-Tribune,* the Cincinnati *Post,* the New York *Globe, The Critic and Guide,* and many other papers and magazines can print and are printing to-day dazes and terrifies the standpatters of morals and sociology, but it joyfully amazes those of us who remember what conditions were thirty, twenty, ten, five years ago.

"Yea, it is no exaggeration to say that many of these editors and business managers would not have consented one year ago to the appearance of such plain writing in the columns of their publications. Would that our friend could have lived one year longer than he did! It would greatly have cheered and comforted him to realize something of the cumulative and transforming effects of his decades of struggle for the spreading of the light. The tiny taper that others had lit went nearly out many times in the centuries of storm; he and his contemporaries bound other tapers with it and the feeble blaze quickened a little and enlarged. At last it became torch and kindling for the black fuel in the furnaces where is generated the active power that throws the light of millions of incandescents and arcs into the secret places of vice, disease, and slavery, and brings into high relief on the columns of righteous fame the names of the men and women who in poverty and misconception and persecution labored and suffered and died that this morning of partial understanding and nascent justice might come to the world. And among those names is that of the man for whom we who contribute to this Memorial bring words of appreciation and loving memory, Edward Bond Foote."

ADDRESS BY

DR. JOHN LOVEJOY ELIOT

(Of the Society for Ethical Culture)

"The philanthropy of Dr. Foote had this vital characteristic of philanthropy: it was absolutely genuine. In these days when so many are giving because it will in some way advance their own interests, in some way redound to their own credit, it is nothing less than inspiring to find the record of a man who gave with no notion of any benefit that he would receive, gave sincerely for the sake of the cause to which he made the donation, and not for his own sake.

"When one reads over the long list of his benefactions, another important fact is brought to light—the great variety of his interests. He was not a man who simply had a 'pet charity,' who was interested in building up a single institution to the exclusion of all other causes. To be sure, it was mostly to liberal institutions that he made gifts. If he had a single cause at heart it may be said that it was that of liberty. It was at the shrine of liberty that he worshiped and to that altar he brought his gifts. In his offerings to liberty, both of his means and his time, he has set for us all a shining mark. Those of us who have borne even a very humble part in this great cause must feel both for ourselves and for that cause a deep sense of loss in the death of this man.

"Those of us who have hoped with Lincoln that 'The time may come when the burden would be lifted from the shoulders of men and all would have an equal chance,' those of us who have seen the burden upon the shoulders of others and have felt it upon our own, must indeed feel deeply the loss of such a comrade, friend, co-worker and leader in the cause of liberty and free speech, and it is well for us to come together here to-day and for our own sake to remember him that we may be inspired to keep alive his fight.

"The question always comes to my mind at such a time, 'What should we do for those who have gone before?' What *can* we do? Our hands are so feeble, our time is so brief, our power is so limited. It seems to me, however, that there is one thing that we can do. We can endeavor to understand those who have gone, even better after they have gone than ever we did in life—to see them again in memory, to let the true effect of their lives come home to us, to believe in them more loyally than we ever did before.

"If there is anything that we can do it is just this, to keep in touch with them and with the eternal truths of life. And we ought not to go away from here without being strengthened in the holy cause of liberty, without having our sympathy, our understanding, our generosity, our faithfulness rekindled by the memory of Dr. Foote."

ADDRESS BY

REV. WILLIAM THURSTON BROWN

"I did not know Dr. Foote personally, as I suppose those did who have preceded me; and yet I sometimes think and feel that I knew him very well, although my only acquaintance with him was through a little correspondence in 1910.

"After leaving the Unitarian Church in which I had hoped to do work which did not depend upon tradition—liberal work—I organized in Salt Lake City the Modern School, naming it after the work of Ferrer. When Dr. Foote learned of this venture in Salt Lake City, he voluntarily sent me his check. There was an unusual cheer and inspiration in his communications, in his letters.

"I was deeply impressed by the address made at the beginning of this meeting by perhaps the oldest man on the platform, the oldest representative of the Free Thought movement here in New York. The thing which he was thinking about was, What is to come of all this? What are we going to do? Where are the men to come from and where are the means to come from which shall carry on the work which has been in other hands hitherto? There is in that suggestion, to my mind, the one thing which can at all justify this meeting, or any other meeting, giving tribute to Dr. E. B. Foote. We can do him no good by what we say about him here. We do ourselves good, to be sure, by what we say, by what we think; and it is a good thing for us even in this inadequate way to express some appreciation of what he did.

"But the only way, the only lasting way, the only sure way in which we can pay any tribute to him is by continuing the work for which he stood. The man goes, but the whole situation of the Free Speech, Free Thought movement remains, and it is only by facing this situation and dealing with it, that we can show that we are sensitive to the deeper and finer meaning of Dr. Foote's life, of this whole movement and that we are responsive to every phase of it. Dr. Foote did not insist that a man or woman should represent only that which bore high repute, nor only that for which he himself had stood; he recognized a Free Thinker under no particular label. And I think the time is coming when the work of the Free Thought Society will be carried out. Emma Goldman has spoken splendid words and has done splendid work for Free Thought, Free Speech. There is no question about that, and we should be proud to recognize it. And yet at the same time it seems to me that there is room and place and need to do more, to build a platform upon which there shall be entire Freedom, upon which there shall be no necessity of omitting this or that or the other phase of freedom. That is the way, or one of the ways, in which we can really pay our tribute to the man who stood for freedom of every phase.

"Free Thought is not Dr. Foote's cause at all, and if we say it or think it to be Dr. Foote's cause we mistake It is the cause of humanity, the cause of the school children of New York City, the cause of this city and of other cities; the cause of the emancipation of the poor devils of all sorts who are in enslavement of any kind. Only as we see the cause in its true light can we do the work which shall really show that we mean what we say when we pay our tribute to Dr. Foote.

"I attended a memorial meeting, or rather a centenary meeting, in honor of Lincoln in Salt Lake City in 1909. I think most of you will agree with me as I sum up the impressions which I received from that meeting or from the two principal speakers at that meeting. One of them was a lawyer, who thought more of precedent than he did of equity. He did not say one single word from beginning to end about equity, but if Lincoln stood for anything as a lawyer he stood for equity. That was the side of the law that he was interested in. Now this man was there as the friend of Lincoln, as an intimate associate of Lincoln. He had lived with him in Springfield, Ill., and yet apparently knew him less than any other man on the platform. He had seen the man nominated at Chicago, in 1860, but he did not say that Lincoln was nominated by a political machine that was just as rotten as any other, and he did not say a thing that gave us light on the natural Lincoln.

"Another of the principal speakers was the Governor of the State—a man who was a political tool, a stand-patter and one who could be used by the unscrupulous politicians of the State. Neither of these men could say anything about Lincoln. They did not know the real Lincoln. It was not a memorial to Lincoln. Only men who were in sympathy with Lincoln could know the man; only such men could pay any tribute to him. And so I say to-day we can honor Dr. Foote only as we feel the same large interest which he felt; only as we see clearly and feel deeply the facts and problems of society about us, the vital issues in sympathetic response to which his life became a benediction and a blessing."

Theodore Schroeder, author, and attorney for the Free Speech League, also spoke at this Memorial Meeting as well as upon a similar occasion before the Brooklyn Philosophical Society, and elsewhere. The substance of his remarks is incorporated in the opening paper of this volume. From the many letters written at the time of Dr. Foote's death and upon the occasion of the Memorial Meeting, the following extracts have been culled.

A LETTER FROM MARY F. WATKINS

It was my privilege during many years to act as amanuensis for the late Edward Bond Foote, and for his father, Edward Bliss Foote. This association gave me an insight into their principles and life work, which I could have obtained in no other way, and every day was an education in itself. I have always felt an inexpressible gratitude that such privilege was mine.

In the Foote family album there was a small photo portrait of Doctor Ned, as he was familiarly addressed, taken when he was a lad of eleven or twelve years. The picture represents him standing, and at first sight gave me then the impression of unusual manliness in the child, and ever after, when I chanced to see it. His countenance at that early age was an unerring index to the character of the man of mature years. Throughout his life the manliness was prominent.

From my earliest remembrance of Dr. Foote his life was one of eternal vigilance in the cause nearest his heart; that of uprooting superstition, and the preservation of individual liberty. He kept in constant touch with the transactions of Congress and the State Legislature, so that when attempts were made to pass laws interfering with freedom of speech, press and mails, he put his whole heart and soul into the fight to defeat all such Legislation. He stood boldly for medical freedom and strongly opposed any movement suggestive of a doctors' trust.

While others slept or played, he was frequently working far into the night, giving his thought to his professional business, and to the liberal work which engaged so much of his time and attention.

His strong sense of justice led him always to the defense of the oppressed. In the light of circumstances as they appeared to him, his judgment was always just. He saw the needs of humanity with a clear breadth of vision that not one in a thousand could approach. His ideals were so far in advance of the average individual, that in future generations his name will be written in letters of gold, as one who loved his fellow men.

Personally, he was modest, and absolutely free from ostentation and pretense of any kind. His habits of industry, thrift, and economy, combined with a sympathetic and generous nature, resulted in the management of his affairs so that when a tale of distress appealed to him, as often happened, he always gave financial assistance to the unfortunate one. While many were appreciative and worthy, unscrupulous people sometimes imposed upon him. A plausible talker could always hold his attention, and, being the embodiment of sincerity himself, the insincerity of others was not readily apparent to him.

His mode of living was very simple; he was content with just enough of the comforts of life, without indulging in anything like follies or extravagances. Of the small vices so common to men in general, he had none. His genial personality, expressed in a keen sense of humor, attracted to him many friends. In his play days at Larchmont, he liked to invite friends to share his pleasures, and he never cared to drive or sail alone.

There was a strong bond of affection between father and son. In troubled moments, he was his father's staunch supporter and comforter.

I remember calling at his city home about a year ago, to see him, and found him resting on a couch, very weak looking, and feeling discouraged. He said he felt himself losing ground. Mrs. Foote, whose untiring devotion anticipated his every wish, was in and out; and as she passed from the room, he turned to me and said, with much tenderness of expression: "She is a great little woman!"

As he grew weaker, he faced the inevitable with the calm cheerfulness of a brave soul, and he remained a philosopher to the end.

A LETTER FROM LILLIAN HARMAN

"My personal recollections of the interest manifested by Dr. Foote in the work of Moses Harman and *Lucifer* extend back to my young girlhood in the early eighties. I think both father and son were subscribers almost from the first issue. I used to read their *Health Monthly* which they sent my father, and I remember reading, at the age of thirteen, "Plain Home Talk," a present to my father from the author—which work has had a great influence on my life to this day. Both doctors were always very friendly to *Lucifer,* but after the cessation of the publication of the *Health Monthly* they seemed almost 'silent partners' in the publication of the paper—so warm was their interest, so ready their words of cheer and their financial assistance. In all the years of government persecution they were stanch supporters of my father, and it is hard to realize that the hands that penned the letters lying before me can never write again.

"It is almost impossible to dissociate Dr. Foote, Sr., and Dr. Foote, Jr., in my mind. In their letters, when one wrote, he always spoke for the other, too. Their professional work brought them into contact with thousands of ruined lives which could have been saved by knowledge of the laws of sex, and so they worked together and welcomed and encouraged every struggling emissary of enlightenment.

"In '86 Dr. Ned wrote his little book, 'The Radical Remedy in Social Science.'

" 'We want,' he says, 'a sufficient education in the science of private and public hygiene and morals, and especially in the direction of sex, reproduction and heredity, which shall be so general that every man and woman at the age of puberty shall know enough, and be religiously inclined, to guard against crippling himself or herself, the family or society, by indulging in vice of any kind, and particularly that of reckless propagation.

" 'That is the *radical remedy,* a thorough one, and Utopian enough for the most devout optimist. Even though it be an electric beacon in whose bright light we may not hope to bask, as 'neath the noonday sun, yet for us its dim rays already show the way to brighter days, and point out the line of progress we should pursue.'

"This book had a wide circulation, and surely had its influence on the thought of our time. The world is coming his way now. His remedy does not seem so startling as it did in '86. A few years later, when I first met Dr. Ned, he took me for a drive through the country lanes near his Larchmont home, and past the Paine Monument—a well-known object of his interest and solicitude.

"He told me the story of the writing of the 'Radical Remedy.' He said he felt at the time that he had only a few months to live, and that this message was the most important legacy he could leave and so devoted his remaining strength to this work. He astonished himself by continuing to live, but he still felt that the work outlined in his 'Radical Remedy' was the most important that he or any one else could do.

"Again, nine years ago, on my last visit to New York, we passed over the same road and talked of the years and the work that had intervened. He said the only occasion for surprise was that he had lived so long and—as he expressed it—accomplished so little. No one who knew him needs to be told of his excessive modesty. Death, he said, was twenty years overdue; it was astonishing that it had delayed so long, but that would surely be our last drive, for when I again came East he would be gone. When I went in and talked with his invalid father, I asked if Dr. Ned's self-diagnosis was correct, and he replied that while Dr. Ned was certainly correct as to his organic disease, he could probably live to old age if he but thought so. 'Ned's temperament,' he said, 'was inherited from his mother, not from me, my temperament being sanguine.'

"But though expressing the opinion that life would soon cease, he did not seem at all depressed. He wanted to make the best of his time and opportunities. In his letters he would sometimes express the opinion that some ruling the courts had made, rendered further fight useless or impossible.

" 'They have you bottled up,' he would write, and would inclose a check, maybe for ten, maybe for a hundred dollars, to help to continue the fight.

" 'Our light is so small and flickering in the wilderness of barbarism,' he once said, 'that I often think it is not worth while for men like Moses—precious few anyway—to suffer for the little that can be done through such martyrdom. But since he is built that way and would rather be where he is than out wearing a padlock, we can't make him over. I must confess they could padlock me all over before I would take his medicine.' But we who know him know that, had the occasion arisen, he would never have submitted to the padlock! . . . . .

A LETTER FROM JULIA H. SEVERENCE, M. D.

"I deeply regret being unable to be with you bodily as I am in spirit this evening to join you in voicing our appreciation of the great loss we suffer in the departure of our comrade and co-worker, Dr. E. B. Foote.

"Dr. Foote was the most modest all-round reformer I ever knew. During the many years I have known him, he has ever been ready to work with voice, pen and purse for the furtherance of any cause that would help in human development. We shall greatly miss his genial presence in our battle for liberty. Who will fill the vacancy in our ranks caused by his departure? I congratulate the doctor, however, on his release from a long and painful illness.

A LETTER FROM M. FLORENCE JOHNSON

"I wish it were possible for me to express my appreciation of Dr. Foote, and his work for humanity, especially his work for children; striving for a condition in which children should be welcome and well born, if born at all. This he did not treat as wholly a woman question, but rather a race question—the perfecting of progeny through both father and mother.

"He helped carry on the work that makes all individuals strive for self-betterment and a knowledge that will eventually leave no woman question, no 'What is woman's sphere? What is man's place in the world?' but 'Here! what can we do for the world,' and each do all in his or her power in one great sphere of work.

"I thank him,

A LETTER FROM JAMES B. ELLIOTT

"Secretary Thomas Paine National Historical Association."

"I wish to add my tribute to the many others that I know will be made at the meeting this morning to Dr. E. B. Foote, a worthy son of a good father, and who inherited the good principles and sound mind of his parents. It was but natural that he should admire the talents and character of Thomas Paine, in which he took a deep interest.

"As the treasurer of the Thomas Paine National Historical Association, in 1905, I met his father, and later, when Mr. Schroeder, the secretary of the Association, resigned, Dr. Foote wrote me, asking me to come and see him and talk over the situation. As a result, I became the secretary of the National Association, which necessitated a constant correspondence with Dr. Foote which continued until a short time before his death.

"In the Paine Museum at New Rochelle, he took a special interest; situated as it was a short distance from Larchmont, his summer residence. He visited it in good weather and looked after its interests, and was always present at the meetings and at the celebrations, and his purse and pen went together to help render tardy justice to the memory of Thomas Paine.

"My last meeting with Doctor 'Ned,' as he was lovingly called at New Rochelle, was when I presented the portrait of Gen. Bonniwell to the Paine Homestead. This idea of having the former owner of the Paine House —and an heir of Thomas Paine—was pleasing to Dr. Foote and he insisted that I should tell him how I resurrected this forgotten portrait from oblivion and restored it to its proper place. He was much interested in the presentation address, and we talked over the possibility of further donations.

"The Association is very much indebted to Dr. Foote for the use of his offices as a meeting place for the annual elections. My relations with the president and members of the Association have been pleasant and I could not help thinking, as I looked upon all that remained of our late treasurer, how I would miss his warm welcome, pleasant smile and hearty handshake when I again visit New Rochelle, but I know he will be with us in spirit and will rejoice to see the Paine Museum grow; he regarded it as a memorial that would outlast marble or bronze and cannot die.

"I can only add in conclusion, as most appropriate, the lines that appeared in the New York *Advertiser,* announcing the death of Thomas Paine, June, 1809:

" 'Take him, for all and all,
We ne'er shall look upon his like again.'

A LETTER FROM FRANKLIN STEINER

". . . . . It was with great regret that I read in to-day's (October nineteenth) *Truth*

Seeker of the death of Dr. Ned Foote. It was not unexpected, as some months ago I was informed that the condition of his health was such as to preclude recovery. In the passing away of the treasurer of three Free Thought associations we have lost one of our most valuable active workers. I knew him well, and am proud to record the fact that he was one of my earliest acquaintances among the prominent Freethinkers of the United States. I cannot help but associate his name with that of his honored father, Dr. Edward Bliss Foote, who passed from life but six years ago. I feel sure that two more splendid men never lived. Their influence on all occasions was for Free Thought, for Free Speech, for the spread of knowledge and of liberty; and for the salvation of man, through the spread of intelligence, the only true saviour, from the ills which beset him.

"I recall the time, in the fall of 1895, when the elder Dr. Foote entertained the late Samuel P. Putnam and myself at his beautiful home in Larchmont, within a stone's throw of the waves of Long Island Sound. It is certainly one of the most precious treasures in my memory. Not the least of his kindnesses was the drive to New Rochelle to visit Thomas Paine's house and monument. Dr. Foote and Mr. Putnam were greatly concerned lest the property should be sold to someone who would pull down the house and remove the monument. Happily Dr. E. B., Jr., lived to see all fear of this set aside by the purchase of the ground around the monument by the city of New Rochelle, and its being turned into a park; and of the house by the Huguenot Association, and now used as a Paine museum. It would be stating an untruth were I to say that the loss of Dr. Ned Foote leaves a gap to be filled without difficulty. His voice, pen and purse were always freely given to every cause for the betterment of humanity, now and here. Gods in the skies to him were matters of indifference; but better, healthier men and women in this world and this world a better world than the world of old—free from ignorance, superstition, bigotry and disease—and glorified by liberty, intelligence, knowledge and human brotherhood, were to him matters of the greatest importance and worthy of the bravest effort. This is the greatest tribute that can be paid to any mortal; and because of that we honor ourselves by keeping green the memory of such noble men as Edward Bond Foote. . . . . .

LETTER FROM CELIA B. WHITEHEAD

". . . . . Being so far away, the sad news of our loss reached me only a short time ago. With much sorrow I read of the passing of an old-time friend and comrade.

"In the passing away of Dr. E. B. Foote, Jr., another generation loses a great man. It was my privilege to have the personal acquaintance of both the doctors, father and son, for several years. I shall always feel that my life is richer for having known them.

"They were very different in personal appearance, but strikingly alike in character; so much so that in writing of the one I seem also to be writing of the other. Kind, tolerant, patient, hospitable, fearless, honest, earnest—what good word is there that I may not say of them?

"Away back in 1878, when I first knew them, the elder was 'Dr. Foote,' and the other a tall, pale, quiet young man—hardly more than a boy he seemed to me—with large, calm, observant eyes, a forehead broad, high and white, and a voice, smile and manner of wonderful charm and sympathy.

"As we were interested in many of the same questions, it was often my privilege and pleasure to contribute to *Dr. Foote's Health Monthly*. Though we often differed in our views, very widely sometimes, never once was I made to feel that my contributions were unwelcome or that I might not have the fullest liberty of expression. Free Speech has lost a brave and able defender; and we need them so much in these days.

"With earnest and honest advocacy of what he believed, our friend combined a rare hospitality for the opinions of those who differed from him; and, seemingly free from all prejudice, asked only: What is truth? More than once, when I indulged in harsh or impatient criticism of those who did not do or think as I thought they ought, I have been made ashamed of my intolerance by the calm and gentle words of Dr. Foote. I cannot remember that I ever heard an unkind word from either the elder or the younger.

"This memento would be very incomplete without mention of the thoroughly democratic spirit of our comrade. To my seeming, he always regarded wealth and station as trivial incidents, scarcely noticed.

"Always unobtrusive, he was never backward where he could be of use. I cannot imagine the Manhattan Liberal Club without his benign presence. But it is many years since I have been there, so possibly there is some one else who can fill his place.

"I saw Dr. Foote only once after leaving the East twelve years ago. I was then in deep grief, and found much comfort in his gentle sympathy, as I am sure everyone did who ever went to him in trouble.

"These things are not set down in the careful order such a subject deserves, because I feared that in this age of hurry the time might go by till I should be too late for any timely expression of my appreciation. I have written of him as he seemed to me. If he had faults I did not see them.

"Will *The Truth Seeker* allow me to express the hope that some time, somewhere, it may again be given to me to meet this grand and beautiful soul who has lately gone from our sight?

A LETTER FROM JOHN PECK

". . . . . It seems to me as though I am entitled to the privilege of saying something for Dr. Foote. I was pained to learn of his death; it seemed to me like parting with a near friend. From personal experience I knew him to be a kind, considerate and benevolent man. He did not reach extreme old age, but his life was eminently useful. He found happiness in promoting the happiness of others, and those who follow his example will not go far astray. Like Ingersoll he tried to smooth down the rough and disagreeable places of life, and make it a little more enjoyable for those who come after. He did not believe in misery here in order to secure happiness hereafter. He was the friend of the true and good; but the designing, selfish and vicious found little favor in his sight. He was a lover of freedom, and above all held in utter abhorrence ecclesiastical shackles. I have never met him, but have a good reason for being thankful for his friendship and generosity. He will always hold a warm place in my heart, and in the hearts of all who knew him. He lived a good life and left the world with a clean record. His memory will be cherished by all who appreciate a noble manhood.

FROM THE TRUTH SEEKER

Death of Dr. Foote

"Dr. E. B. Foote, Jr.—Doctor Ned—died at his home, 120 Lexington Avenue, New York, on Saturday, October twelfth. The event was expected, for it has been many months since Dr. Foote lost the use of his limbs and became a 'shut-in,' but that fact does not lessen the sadness of the announcement. A trouble that began in what he called 'neuritis,' but was probably due to blood-poisoning contracted many years ago as a medical student, gradually extended from the hands to all parts of the body, until paralysis became general, and little of the sufferer retained animation except the brain. *The Truth Seeker* received a letter from him but a few days ago which was perhaps the last he dictated.

"Dr. Edward Bond Foote was born on August fifteenth, fifty-eight years ago, near Cleveland, Ohio, his father being Edward Bliss Foote, a native of Ohio, and his mother, Catherine G. Foote, a New England school teacher. The elder Foote was for thirty years actively interested in Liberal work, and the son's history during that time was identical with the father's. They were members of the National Liberal League and organizers of the National Defense Association. It has been said of Doctor Ned that he was theoretically an opponent and practically an opposer of all the principal restrictions on life, liberty, and the pursuit of happiness; that he did not believe in compulsory vaccination, or the suppression of undiplomaed healers, or postoffice censorship, or interference with liberty of the press, nor in laws governing the moral or religious character of matter transported by common carriers, nor in the concealment of any kind of physiological knowledge. And all that he believed in he advocated, and all that he did not believe in, of a character affecting rights and liberties, he worked against with voice and pen and money and influence. He helped everybody who was working in the same field. He was an officer in all of the Liberal societies of New York, as president, secretary, or treasurer—usually the last, for he inherited his father's business capacity, and like him was a man of means and a liberal giver. At the time of his death he was treasurer of the American Secular Union, of the Free Speech League, and of the National Thomas Paine Historical Association. He was first treasurer of the Francisco Ferrer Association. Nobody but himself knew how much of his means he devoted to his friends in forward movements, or in adversity. He began public speaking before he was out of the Medical College, and gave many lectures before the Manhattan Liberal Club. He was a good writer, practical and full of sane suggestions, and always in even temper. His sense of humor was acute, and a good joke went as far in enlisting his sympathies as a tale of woe, for he responded to both. He forgot nobody, even those who might not think themselves worthy of being held in mind, and was perpetually surprising them with his remembrances. There would be no bad people in the world if he could have bribed them all to be good. Some eight years ago he asked the writer to prepare a brief sketch of his, Dr. Foote's, life for a publication that was issuing. He said he wanted it honest and truthful, and we consented with the understanding that he should do an 'obituary' for us when the proper time arrived.

"His was a life that will bear the light.

There is nothing to conceal or to overlook. He had the qualities that make up the superior specimens of the human family. He was one of the best men we ever knew, and if he had any faults we never detected them or heard them named. A rare gift to humanity was Doctor Ned—a gift for which no equivalent remains now that it is withdrawn, except the memory of one who was always loyal, always generous, always helpful, and ever the soul of cheerfulness and the cup of strength."

"The attendants at the funeral of Dr. E. B. Foote, October sixteenth, crowded the rooms of the double house at 120 Lexington Avenue, the historic home of the Footes, where the services were held. In dwindled numbers the Old Guard who knew the doctor as a boy came there to bury him. Joseph Warwick, the oldest of them, with his eighty-three years, and David Hoyle, two years his junior, were present. Thaddeus B. Wakeman, nearing seventy-nine, served to recall the many occasions when he, as not on this occasion, spoke the last word. David Rousseau, aged but stalwart, might have met and saluted young Ned Foote in his sailboat on the Sound thirty years since. Dr. Charles Andrews and his family had 'always' known him. Mrs. Mary Watkins, who as Miss Smith wrote the elder Dr. Foote's letters two decades ago and after, seemed the surviving member of Foote and Son. Edwin C. Walker, who has known Dr. Ned ever since he needed a friend, could bear first-hand testimony to his devotion to liberty of press and mails. In the younger crowd was Edward Dobson, who as an employee of *The Truth Seeker* in the '90s must have mailed away many copies of Dr. Foote's books, and who, after getting literary instruction in this office, is now the telegraph editor on a big daily. And there were the ruddy and golden youths, Leonard Abbott and James Morton, and the battle-scarred old soldier of the cooperative commonwealth, C. P. Somerby. Gilbert Roe, Esq., was the doctor's colleague in the Free Speech League, as was Theodore Schroeder.

We saw Mrs. Sterling and Mrs. Cone and Rachel Andrews and Maude Ingersoll among the women. The employees of the Murray Hill Publishing Company, of which Dr. Foote was the head, made a considerable group, and the charitable and benevolent associations to the support of which he was contributor probably were represented by persons unknown to the Liberal world. On a mantel stood a photograph of Ned from which was made the half-tone in Putnam's 'Four Hundred Years of Freethought.' It looked as he did that year we shifted sandbags for him on his boat that was in the Larchmont regatta, and when he could make somersault dives from a springboard. We forget the name of the boat, but recall the winning, the jubilation and the dinner where ginger ale flowed like champagne. It is a satisfying picture, with its associations, and so we did not glance with the others at the wasted face in the elongated coffin among the wreaths. We could hear but a part of the funeral discourse by John Lovejoy Eliot of the Society for Ethical Culture, to which we are told Dr. Foote belonged. Those who heard it say that, knowing Dr. Foote, they could trace his likeness in Dr. Eliot's delineation of his life and character.

Only members of the Old Guard followed the hearse to the crematory. The mechanism of the catafalque moved inexorably and in unbroken silence, save from the organ strains; that part of our friend which was visible and which we have lost passed behind the closed doors of the retort; and, somewhat stunned, the spectators turned away. It was a double farewell that was paid that day—a farewell to Dr. Ned Foote, and good-bye to the house at 120 Lexington Avenue where they have met for the last time in council. Dr. Foote survived his two brothers, and neither he nor they left offspring to bear the family name, which is gone."

FROM THE FREETHINKER

London, England, November 8, 1912

" . . . . Dr. Foote will never be forgotten by those who knew him. In my own memory he will always occupy a peculiar place. . . . . . His was a beautiful and generous spirit, without vice of any kind. He was not even personally ambitious. Selfishness and vanity had no part in him. He was a born giver; his generosity was known from New York to San Francisco and he often sent me donations for the work here which he would not even allow me to acknowledge publicly. . . . Lack of physical vitality which nature showers lavishly on pigs and fools, lent a certain appearance of frustration to his life. Nature so often treats her elect in this way that perhaps I may well close this tribute to my friend with those lines of Swinburne's:

" 'For thee, O now a silent soul, my brother,
Take at my hands this garland, and farewell.
Thin is the leaf and chill the wintry smell,
A chill the solemn earth—a fatal mother,
With sadder than the Niobean womb,
And in the hollow of her breasts a tomb.
Content thee, howsoe'er, whose days are done;
There lies not any troublous thing before,
Nor sight nor sound to war against thee more,
For whom all winds are quiet as the sun,
All waters as the shore.' "

FROM MOTHER EARTH

"In the death of Dr. Edward B. Foote the radical movement has lost one of its staunchest friends.

"While the main interest of Dr. Foote centered in Free Thought and Free Press along the lines of sex enlightenment, he never failed to take a broad-minded stand in behalf of everything pertaining to free expression. He differed from the average liberal in that he was a firm and active believer in Free Speech even for those with whom he did not agree. Whether it was a question of arrested participants in a Czolgosz meeting, or a Free Speech fight in Spokane, San Diego or some other place, Dr. Foote could always be relied upon for his sympathy, and for his moral and financial assistance.

"Though not an Anarchist, he was a most generous and devoted friend to *Mother Earth* and to the work carried on by our little group. We mourn his death, however, not because of his generosity to us, but because with him departed a man who *really* believed in freedom of speech—for everyone, including those whom he considered in the wrong. Still more do we mourn his death because of the fact that there are few, very few, young Americans to take the place of men like Dr. Edward B. Foote."

FROM THE MALTHUSIAN

November 15, 1912

"We deeply regret to hear that Dr. Edward B. Foote, our constant supporter in the United States, died on Saturday, October twelfth last, at his home at 120 Lexington Avenue, New York. Dr. Foote was a warm and consistent advocate of all advanced humanitarian causes, and the list of societies in which he took an active interest is a formidable one. In the New York *Herald* in which the announcement of his death appeared mention is made of his connection with the Association for Practical Housekeeping, the Men's League for Women's Suffrage, the Berkshire Farm Association, New York Probation Association, Brooklyn Bureau of Charities, Parks and Playgrounds Association, Children's Aid Society, Prison

Association of New York, National Purity Association, Society for Ethical Culture, New Rochelle Hospital, Washington Square House for Friendless Girls, Mothers and Babies Committee of the State Charities Aid Committee, Child Labor Committee, Brooklyn Affiliated Charities, American Seamen's Friend Society, Postal Reform League, and the Charity Organization Society. . . . . .

"At a meeting of the Council of the Malthusian League, held on Thursday, November seventh, the following resolution was unanimously passed.

" 'The Council of the Malthusian League has heard with the deepest regret of the death of Dr. Edward B. Foote, and desires to record the obligation of the Neo-Malthusian movement to him for his teaching and support. It tenders its heartfelt sympathy to Mrs. Foote in her bereavement.' "

FROM THE TRUTH SEEKER

November 2, 1912

Dr. Ned Foote

"Under the paralyzing sense of loss in the death of Dr. Edward B. Foote, it is impossible to prepare a formal eulogy. His personality was too broad, too sweet, too lovable, to allow the ordinary conventional tribute. A hater of empty ceremonialism, and in every moment of his life a consistent lover of straightforward simplicity, he would not have willed that any of his friends should speak of him other than as the heart might prompt. He did not directly fight conventionality; he simply lived beyond and above it. Even long after the death of his father, it pleased him to be referred to by the tenderly familiar name of Doctor Ned. He was at all times approachable even by those having no claim whatever on his exceedingly valuable time. To every suggestion, however impracticable, and to every request, however unreasonable, he listened with the same unvarying kindness and thoughtful consideration. His denial, rarely heard where even a grain of merit could be detected by him, was more kindly and gentle than the consent of most men would be, and was invariably tempered by some spontaneous word or act of help. How many individuals have been helped by him over tight places, or saved from utter ruin by his unequaled generosity, will never be known or even guessed. His public beneficences were enormous, and probably bulked larger in proportion to his income than the donations of any other well-to-do Liberal in the land. It has always been impossible to learn their aggregate, as his extreme modesty insisted on anonymity in the case of a great number of them. Great as they were, however, it is doubtful whether they were not overtaken and passed by his countless gifts and practically unreturnable loans to particular persons in need of help. His nature seemed wholly composed of kindness; and he found no pleasure in life comparable to that of bringing brightness into the world by fruitful acts of helpfulness to persons or to causes.

"It is impossible to conceive of any person knowing Dr. Foote, even slightly, and not loving him. This expression, often redolent of sloppy sentimentality, is the only one that fits in his case. He radiated a peculiar sweetness, which I have marked in but two or three other men among the thousands whom I have known, one of them being his universally loved father, from whom he derived a double portion of that rare attribute. There was not, it need scarcely be said, the slightest trace of effeminacy in his nature. His gentleness involved no lack of virility, as all can testify who have seen his eye flash with noble indignation, and have heard his voice ring out in energetic manly protest against some act of public or private iniquity. Of all forms of evil, he most abhorred any wilful attempt to hold human beings in ignorance. Among the many causes to which he devoted his energies and his money, none was closer to his heart than the fight for Free Speech in its every phase. To my personal knowledge, there were occasions when he deeply regretted the course taken by certain victims of persecution, and found himself in complete and emphatic opposition to their entire point of view and the methods pursued by them. This, however, never caused him to waver a hair's breadth in the ardor with which he fought to secure for them the full right of expression which he claimed for himself and for all human beings. No man ever lived who trusted more implicitly the inherent power of truth to justify itself, in the face of the allowance of the freest possible course to even the most multifarious and deadliest errors. He held that the promulgation of the most insidious and infamous doctrine was fraught with immeasurably less evil to humanity than the annihilation of vital human rights involved in its violent suppression by law or by mob rule.

"It would be an error to suppose that Dr. Foote had become a full convert to every movement to which he so generously contributed. With the most progressive views he was indeed in hearty sympathy. But there were many movements, young and in need of encouragement, as to which his judgment remained in reserve. Yet he could see in them the opportunity for human enlightenment on important subjects, and the probability of social progress receiving a measure of stimulus through their agitation. Hence he did not hesitate to assist their ardent defenders to bring more fully to the world the message which they felt prompted to deliver. Unlike many reformers, he did not fail to perceive the need of immediate succor for the victims of fundamental wrongs, while striving with all his might to reach and remove the underlying causes of those wrongs. The partial list of the organizations to which he contributed, which will be found in a former issue of *The Truth Seeker,* well illustrates his practical realization of the balance to be kept among the many forms of activity for the public welfare.

"When all these things have been said,

there is still no adequate expression of the heaviness which lies on the hearts of a multitude who do not easily yield to emotion. The friend whom we mourn was not a mere nexus of altogether desirable qualities, to which we may pay tribute in carefully chosen words. He was a warm, living personality, belonging so intimately to our lives that it is hardly possible to believe that he is really gone. It seems impossible to spare one whose place can never be taken by another. He was a man of men, perhaps the truest of soul and highest of purpose whom I have ever known. Death came to him as a release from extreme physical suffering. He lies at rest, 'a portion of the loveliness which once he made more lovely'; and our only fitting tribute to his memory must be to carry on to a larger triumph the work for y which was all of life to him.

DEATH OF EDWARD B. FOOTE.

Louis F. Post, United States Commissioner of Labor in an editorial in The Public said:

"In the death on the twelfth of Dr. Edward B. Foote of New York, progressive movements have lost one of their most loyal supporters. His devotion began with his youth; it never slackened until his death. With some of his activities The Public was not in sympathy, but Dr. Foote's truly democratic spirit which inspired them all, and was as a steady light in a dark place, could not fail to command universal respect. He served not only causes that were popular, but also and with even more intensity many that were yet in their swaddling clothes and their mangers, or in process of crucifixion. The popu-

CPSIA information can be obtained
at www.ICGtesting.com
Printed in the USA
LVOW04s1328020216
473340LV00023B/666/P